just between us

just between us

david mcelroy

UNIVERSITY OF ALASKA PRESS FAIRBANKS

Text © 2018 University of Alaska Press

Published by
University of Alaska Press
P.O. Box 756240
Fairbanks, AK 99775-6240

Cover and interior design by Kristina Kachele Design, llc.

Cover and author photo by Edith Barrowclough.

Library of Congress Cataloging in Publication Data

Names: McElroy, David, author.
Title: Just between us / David McElroy.
Description: [Fairbanks, Alaska] : University of Alaska Press, [2018] |
Identifiers: LCCN 2017028638 (print) | LCCN 2017031229 (ebook) |
ISBN 9781602233515 (ebook) | ISBN 9781602233508 (paper : alk. paper)
Classification: LCC PS3563.A2926 (ebook) | LCC PS3563.A2926 A6 2018 (print) |
DDC 811/.54dc23
LC record available at https://lccn.loc.gov/2017028638

.

For Edie and Brandon

with love

Table of Contents

Acknowledgments

Alaska Quarterly Review
  "Hulling Rice"

Anchorage Daily News
  "Eclipse"

Cirque Journal
"Chipa," "Coccyx," "Ice Road Trucker," "In My Deli Dream," "In Your
Child Soldier Dream," "In Your Snowflake Dream," "Just Between
Us," "Melting Pot," "Morning Paper," "Pachamama," "Pall Bearers,"
"Some Fogs," "Take an Orange in Case You Get Lost," "Ugly Lovers,"
"Videographer," "Volcanoes in the Window," "Weatherman Healing,"
"Zacualpa"

F Magazine
  "In Your Future Dream"

Fairbanks Arts Association Poetry Contest Newsletter
  "Paul Austin: Oilfield Pianist"

Great River Review
"Cheyenne Mountain Zoo," "Encephalogram," "I Got a Sawzall," "In
Your Apple Dream," "In Your Tie Dream"

Ice Floe
"Cruising the Baltic," "In Your Light Dream," "In Your Piano Tuner
Dream," "In Your Sexual Fantasy Dream," "In Your Retirement Dream,"
"Siping," "Three Weeks Rain"

Waiting for You

Pushing a cart in the box store, hiking the Andes,
berry picking the Chugach, or sitting on cardboard
by a Dumpster rattling my cup, someday I'll wait for you
as you jog up in sweats or slouch by in suit and tie.

You might linger to check hair and mascara
in your mirror, retie your bunny boots, if shod,
or spit a wad of betel nut through red gums and filed teeth
before we nod and exchange the guarded hello,

our password, the encrypted chip, this common covenant
that passes from one to another. Then off you go, padding
along barefoot like as not, keys and bangles jangling, erect,
balancing on your head a Clorox urn, all of it so you.

Woven Zigzag with Lightning

Cheyenne Mountain Zoo

The breeding program is successful,
and nineteen giraffes mill in a stately dance
by our tall perch, save for the stud
in a separate paddock who vacations alone.

It's hard to imagine them surviving
on thorn trees. We place hardtack crackers
on their quivering, long blue tongues as cold mountain
shadow dims developments spreading east.

My nearly brother brother-in-law, my son,
his arm-in-arm sweetheart on school break,
and I, today's little family troop, enter
the warmth and sadness of the primate house.

Nearly feeding time, the gibbons are restless.
Baby clings, and mother brachiates, landing
three-handed on the glass for a closer look
at the strange way we have of walking away.

An orangutan preens a partner's genitals.
Through cement walls we hear the lion roar
for his forty pounds of meat. Outside, we see him
on his rock with full dark mane and four spotted cubs—

yes, majestic, damn it, in our cliché.
Next door the Mexican wolves, three brothers,
trot day and night among their penned aspen.
One howls, and we pause in our walk to the car

to better catch the resonant theme and silence
after or maybe answer. So far nothing, and we pass
the tiger, silent Siberian, pacing the prison pines,
then hippos in the hippo house full of potential

standing like propane tanks eating their hay.
Soon enough, love and custom, habits
and hungers, and our successful ways of increase
will bring us home to supper with our kind.

Cruising the Baltic

That sea has no tide,
and barely brackish, few herring,
little salt. Our ship is so big,
twelve stories up you don't reach
a hand for a taste test. Industrial
travel makes waves, but no sound
lapping on the hull can rise this high.

We're so American,
from here streaks
of algae look like oil.
But just like home,
the midnight sun comes up at two,
and the Gulf of Finland
lies flat as a platitude.

Europe lies low to left and right.
Reaching out in six or eight
languages, our city guides
are well-spoken. Living so closely,
they teach war as tides flooding over.
Ironical and right, smallest
countries have the most to say.

Look, sensible cars, smart
and small. The young and old
and ministers of government, slim,
and half of them women, on bikes
in bike lanes riding to work.
Even farmers go to school. Look,
art and flowers and ice cream.

We're heading east, and those birch
on shore are friends of mine,
countrymen who stand together
and don't reach out.
Fireweed blooms familiar,
derelict and magenta on a rusting
freighter listing on a jetty.

Now come cranes, dented
containers, rolls of steel, ingots
of aluminum. Awash at a pier,
a sub is gasping for air.
Nosing in at four, we spot
the lone rower in a tiny boat
pulling hard for Tallinn.

Russia at last
and the town that Peter built.
We see the bear, soiled cub
with a muzzle, held at bay
tied behind a can for coins.
We crowd Catherine's house
scuffing her floral parquet.

Boris, brusque and so Russian,
recites endurance of heroes
of the great city under siege.
Before I can hate him for pushing us
too fast, he soulfully quotes Pushkin
about the Neva wild in flood, lost love,
and the man it drove crazy.

We end up rushed through Peter's
summer place, a fine place for picnics
and wedding pics documenting union:
groom a little drunk, bride laughing,
fountains spouting, statues posing,
and Samson, crazy man so big and gold,
yanking a lion's jaws apart.

Sabrina Bort

The door slides open, and she leans
into our compartment in car eleven
as we roll through small towns and green fields
of formerly East German hay.

"Just checking," she says and hands out
water and lunches in paper sacks.
No clickety-clack, the rails are smooth,
and the hell is gone from sixty years

and thirty years and fifteen years back
for grandparents, parents, and herself
as a kid, prime recruit as a child spy
I imagine for ratting them out to the Stasi.

She does her best to make us couples
into comfortable and organized travelers,
but she is small and elegant with her hair
pulled back, and her beauty is disturbing.

Caramel skin over collar bones,
black scoop-necked top under a white jacket,
on her lapel the tag with number 11
and the continental reach of her name.

Her image is contraband smuggled across
borders of one good marriage after another.
Undulating fields passing, free market cows watching,
she leans this way, and they haven't a clue.

Kriskindlmarkt

I'm slow with jet lag and foggy with a head cold.
The snowy sounds of Vienna arrive muffled
like muttered speech in hotels, the bump and rustle
of doors and drawers, the laundry of Louise and Harold
unpacking opinions next door just passing through.
For all that the streets are festive. The scarved citizens
so worth a second glance are bright and slim.
A shop sign calls out: "Manganese make my color blue."
Glühwein and brats abound in Christmas markets,
and the obligatory Holocaust Memorial in Albertina Square
defaces hate slowly in falling snow that never forgets.
On the library's high cliff, Athena's quadriga rears
over ignorance, seen as two women falling, marble locks
waving, bare breasts blooming, airy swimming, box of rocks.

Bellagio

Five swans and a daw catch my eye—
the swans drifting apart; the daw, squawking
in flight that looks like hard rowing.
The docks extend their arms to any boat
that floats, one ferry after another.
The lake, like a man played with
and ridden on, lies down at night.

Centuries of man and hammer
convinced the mountains to donate
stone we walk on, climbing
sixty-seven steps to where we sleep.
Centuries of women planted, hoed,
milked, and passed on the cooking we ate
today. They made these replacements

walking off boats with a walk
that catches the eye as spike heels
wobble, and landscape becomes
background for cell phones and the flipping,
the flipping of hair. Designer scarves,
wine bars, the talk and texting at every corner
confirm industrial growth for being seen.

Roman legions decamped, and the wine
of late light drains from vineyards. Ciao
to dull competence and governments that work.
We bake no bread, we break no stone,
but here's to the swans who reach a quorum
in the dark. They waddle ashore, graceful,
nonverbal, and stable on their flat black feet.

My First Wat

Two five-headed Naga serpents
fiercely guard the steps up to the wat.
Three three-foot finials swoop
from the triangle of the ornate roof
passionately baroque in the Theravada
way. No humble chapel here, it's a bit
overdone for one who was taught not
to stand out. I'm pleased, though, to note
guests remove their shoes as we at home do.

In the shrubby yard amiable chickens
at peace with their scratching
go about their business
under my first breadfruit tree.

A bird the field guide calls
a red-whiskered bulbul, cocky
as a bullfinch, undulates across
the street where the bamboo culture
lives on. Men climb high scaffoldings
of the stuff building an office tower.

They strap each joint of the poles,
up and across, with split bamboo
and twist them tight with bamboo
sticks lashed with bamboo
cord to keep from untwirling.
A practical art to admire,
all of it bamboo, tight as a nut.

Several stories up a neon sign bolts on.
On it, the script an offshoot of Sanskrit,
angry cursive, has something to do
with something digital.

Higher still, welders balance
on girders, and a million sparks flower
down through this lattice of dry grass.
No harness, goggles, barricades,
in the land of luck no one wears a hard hat.

An ugly dog, part rat, sparse brown hair,
scaly tail, trots across the yard with a vast
and pendulous scrotum flopping wildly.
No need for conquest, he can purchase
the future with genes from his ample purse.

If I were that dog, I would, of course,
walk with pride but never jog.
As it is, I'm a sixty-year-old smiling
private man. But desire being what it is,
a fire triangle of oxygen, heat, and fuel
needs only an ignition source sparking
along in a walk that walks the talk.

I mount the warm stone steps barefoot
with poise, reasonably lucky,
centered, momentarily Buddhist,
modestly hung in the middle way.

Head held high, I sniff the redolent air,
a cocktail more complex than I can fully smell
or name but surely some mix of bruised fruit,
scooter exhaust, and from somewhere fumes
of a stunning mongrel bitch.

Hulling Rice

At two a rooster crows and all hell breaks loose
in brilliant moonlight. All creation's cocks
wake up hysterical in false dawn and shout
hallelujah hallelujah. I curl tighter
in my bag. This can't be the first full moon
in these parts. Soon good chicken sense
prevails, and we all settle down.

At five thirty, moonlight still, one then two
then more crow with better historical reason.
Somewhere across the creek a slow thump,
thump, thump draws me out. In shadows
by a house on stilts on a sloping yard
kept clean by livestock, a woman works
a big log lever with one foot hulling rice.

The far end of the log fits at right angles
into another log, larger around but short.
This hammer is round where it pounds rice
in a hollow stump. Her silhouette steps and steps
on the moonlit log. The rice jumps and jumps,
sliding back for pounding and pounding
in the hard, old elegant design for breakfast.

She scoops kernels and hulls onto a bamboo
tray then flips the contents three moonlit feet
into the mountain breeze flowing across
the Golden Triangle. Kernels fall to the tray for us.
Hull chaff floats to a mat, is swept into a trough,
stirred with water from the creek, and fed
to clucking chickens and a magnificent black pig.

The long trek home begins uphill on trails
small men in black pajamas use to carry
hill rice to market in fifty-kilo sacks.
At home when I eat rice, I think of the woman
in the morning moon, her magnificent black pig
and excitable chickens. So as not to spill one grain
I bow down to fork and bowl wide awake.

Waterfalls

You can't maintain a steady walk by one.
Like setters scenting quail, we round
a descending trail and freeze on point.
Any falls shows near-term failure of erosion.
As in a grand seduction—Anna and Vronsky—
it makes its abrupt statement—No—on a ledge
of weakening resolve. Near Doi Suthep
water falls through arching green exotic
drawing rooms to froth the floor of sediment,
the mounting evidence.
Past mountain swiddens, domestic violence
of slash and burn, our little simile comes
close to metaphors of how we live.
It flows and gathers into the flat brown Ping,
civil and winding through Chiang Mai.
It braids rice paddies sprayed eight
times a year with malathion and so on
into the Chao Phraya, replenishing
and poisoning the Mississippi of,
the Nile of Thailand. It flows
among the klongs of Bangkok
heavy with all it carries from mountain,
plain, and city, at sundown a man bathing,
and into the Gulf of Siam where we swim.

Prayer for the Love Coach

Dear Lord, we ask you to fix their minibus
VW Westfalia camper, home away from home,
this middle-aged couple's coche de la amor.

May they cool in the waterfall while they wait.
May the mechanic's hands drop the motor
gently, may the parts arrive by angels
soon or, more miraculous, by chicken bus.

May the Mayan ruins loom intriguing,
and suffer the dreadlocked twenty-somethings
coming unto them to charm, chat, and to borrow.

Please guide the bolts into their holes and nuts
to be threaded, grease as required, and shim
where needed. And please bless the timing.

We ask that pistons work in congress with spark
and valves, but until then we ask that dogs
and chickens panting in the shade of the bus
be allowed to dream at peace with their fleas.

May the slow journey to see this world resume.
May winding roads be kind. And the travelers,
forgive them for the sugar ants on pastry,
this morning's only protein, which they ate. Amen.

Desert Walk

Armless saguaro too young to wave
much less salute but old enough
for sex open their white flowers
to night and pollinating bats
that might, that must, come by.

Except for grasses, mesquite
and most plants here hang seedpods,
a rich feed ripening for two kinds of doves,
these little rats along the trail,
cottontails, and ducks in the creek.

And so the need for hanging hawks,
owls that burrow, coyotes wafting
like dust through creosote brush,
and in the heat among cactus thorns
snakes sewing the needles of themselves.

Lush rock in low sun, green cattails,
the beat-up tin of water over gravel,
hopeful saguaro ruler straight—
over a hill, around a bend,
the land composes a scene of itself.

And the woman on whom nothing is lost
aims her camera with one hand,
and with the other in complete confidence
passes the cup she's been holding
over her shoulder to the hand
in the desert behind her which is mine.

Pachamama

By the river Mother of God where we sat down
to change our lives, brown water lapped mud.
We'll need a little land. Hand tools, beans, good
books, chickens, and coca leaves for tea at dawn,
a canoe, and eventually an outboard. We'll make time
for friends, speak dialect for bright birds, the calling
out to medicinal plants and the oropendula's falling
song. To stop colds and flu, our common coin,
we'll pay the shaman in corn, fish, and beer.
We'll spill wine on banks of the river Mother of God,
and where morphos flex blue and blue we'll pray to mud.
The fire ant tree grows protected whose friends are fierce.
Bless us now, black caiman. No harm please to river
children bathing and to you, O spangled cotinga, I swear.

Chipa

Rosaria's hands hurt, but rolling the dough
feels good. The low flames
of her fingers flicker with body heat,
melting cheese and lard into manioc flour
sprinkled now and then with coriander.

Manioc, someone dug up the big fat roots,
shredded and soaked them to get the cyanide out—
How many goiters, how much loss to learn this?
Someone washed the death out.
Someone dried and ground the flour

behind the bus station above the creek.
Traffic, sidewalk market, horns, lotto seller
calling out your lucky day. The sun burns
yellow on sweet peppers green and red.
A bus pulls in, a bus pulls out.

Rosaria rolls the dough and sometimes
braids it like a rope, like the heavy sway
of hair on a girl's back roller-skating
away. But today it's shaped as a donut,
ball, or bun and baked on bricks

half an hour at 250 C. Her daughter,
this girl with long black hair charming
your hunger, sings out, "Chipa?"
And you buy it, putting your trust
in the street and the bread of life.

Seven Sleepers in the Street

Three on the corner, four
down the block, their sprawl
outside the colonial church
is pure relief. Take this one,
one foot no kidding in the gutter.

He clutches a coil of rope
in the vice of his hand,
a tumpline with sweat-stained
leather in the middle to strap
the pull of work to his forehead.

Dead away from weight
he's usually tied to, asleep
or drunk, he's not dead yet.
The hollow cheeks puff solemn
to the stubborn pulse of life.

Day dawns chilly on market day.
Families set up booths where benches
bow with bags of beans, corn,
and clothing woven zigzag with lightning,
embroidered with brilliant birds.

Everything here came overnight
on the head of a woman—
gas grill, juicer machine,
baskets of textiles, tortillas, live chickens,
live turkeys, you name it—

Or on the back of a man—
bags of beans, corn, copal,
concrete cinder blocks, carcasses
of beef. A man leans into the ribs
and walks away with half a cow.

Forty years ago I saw the same,
but time has aged the children
we call our future into better health.
Not a runny nose, no eyes of chalk.
Even the dogs look good, and a treaty

currently works. Heaps of shoes,
bundles of lilies, the babble, haggle,
and compromise work like good government.
Women in the market, parents of the present,
we're clicking pictures of your pride.

Heroes of survival easy in the street,
the dreamers look the same, resting
please God where they may. And we who walk
the hills we share soon enough shall find
our beds of cotton, foam, or stone.

But for now the day warms along
on steep streets of golden cobble,
and tonight I'll warm my hand along
your thighs weary from their own work
of bearing from the gutter where they meet
the necessary and the magnificent.

Volcanoes in the Window

Three women half my size help
each other heft bags of sand
at least their weight onto their backs.
With tumplines across their foreheads,
they lean into their steps.
The scuffling of bare feet,
their breath, and the whisper
of handwoven skirts
is all you hear.

With the kind of muscle
that once built pyramids,
all day they haul sand from the beach
of the lake uphill to the expat's house,
five plots bought from locals,
each deed signed with a thumbprint.
The women labor through the gate
of the wall they helped build
to keep themselves out.

Over stones of five homes
men with shovels, not even
a wheelbarrow, mix the sand
with water and cement on the floor
of the what will be the living room.

"Go with Santos. He's honest
and takes care of everything,"
the new owner says
with new owner pride
for the archaeology he's building.

He shows me kitchen counters
with bullnose tile, the terraced yard
with tons of rock work,
irrigation from the village creek.
"They do good work
for which I'm glad to pay
with only here and there a mistake."

You have to admit the view
over the wall of this paradise and the next
takes your breath away.
You have to admit
you can afford this.

Zacualpa

One of the things you have to avoid is
that people try to rewrite the history
books.
—CLYDE SNOW, forensic anthropologist
(*International Miami Herald*, 9 August 1992)

I remember them, the Quiché
watching TV in the institute
vestibule under the stairs.
I remember themes the tapes
promoted: democracy, béisbol,
and a cartoon on personal hygiene
where a Cantinflas look-alike
slinks off into the brush alone
thus illustrating the concept
don't shit in the milpa.

What you smelled working its way
up the stairs was woodsmoke
from cooking fires soaked through
and through their handwoven clothes,
work sweat, baby sweat,
and something somehow sweet,
maybe some mix of breast milk,
cane chicha, and diabetes breath.

How strange I must have appeared
coming down the stairs always
in a hurry shaking a few hands
on my way out to lunch.
How strange so many disappeared
and left the country, as authorities said,
having a good time in Paris or Mexico.

I never saw Zacualpa, those huts
on the mountain, special gardens,
nor the big old church.
I never saw the storage shed
behind the church nor hooks
in the roof as witness to martyrs.

I was far away by then,
baby in my coat,
snowshoeing wild hills
of the North to make him sleep.

But one day the army we trained
comes with civil patrols. On threat
of their own deaths, they arrest
their neighbors. They rope them,
hang them from hooks
to question, beat, blood-splatter
the walls and kill the fear
out of them, cut them down,
mulch them, bury them
in soft soil of the gardens.

Eventually comes harvest,
and I read the forensic report.
"Every skull out of the ground
is one less person living it up in Paris."

I have not seen the hooks
nor how fastened. If nails,
what hammer drove
them straight? If rock, what rock
was there to pound and peen over?
If rope or wire, how looped around
the beams? How roven
through holes and bight,
how snugged, how tied?
If wire, from what fence cut,
and how twisted? If bolts,
what size and arrangement?
How turned by what pliers,
what wrench? And by what hands,
so much like these
that meet and greet and shake
to make hold through pain and time,
neighbor, cousin, and brother,
jolt by living jolt?

In Your Dreams

In Your Piano Tuner Dream

By ten the book shuts the door
in your face. Your eyes close,
head slumps, jaw drops,
and a moth flies out of your mouth
with your soul on its nightly run.

You're riding a Shan pony
down a mossy draw.
Red flowers twist in the mane.
You're hot, but in all this humidity
someone beyond the ranges
needs you, and you're sent for.
In black pajamas your guide
jogs ahead and doesn't break a sweat.

How pianos get where they are
is a common tale of doors
and stairs and workmen's valor.
How hammers complain to the strings
with each jolt along more and more
difficult passages: when the truck
swerves, the elephant slips
on the steep trail, when the left front
porter falls clutching his leg,
dying from the krait strike.
All of it, the contrapuntal fugue
of transport. As if drought and monsoon
weren't enough, no wonder they need you.

You go to work at middle C.
A semitone off, too low,
and the trebles are worse.
From hitch pin to tuning pin,
the tension's gone soft.

For each key, you tighten the middle
string first, then its two side
companions, striking and plucking,
turning out the slack, tuning in
the sharp because soon they'll settle.

You regulate the action, the linkage
between the fingers' touch and sound.
Reaching deep in the belly of the box,
you level the hammers' heights,
free the sticking jack centers,
and tweak the let-off
where the jack kicks out from the hammers.

Enough for now. Perhaps, the pianist
who plays Bach here for warlords
may incite a treaty, sparing
a village and a rape or two
with a well-tempered clavier.
Perhaps even the great Liszt,
coming from his house on Andrassy
Street near Hero Square
swatting bugs would approve.

Soon you'll wake refreshed and wonder
at the lump on your finger, the tuner's
callus. But first the moth
must return with the load of your soul
weary from the best work
it knows. Voicing,
what you do with felts and leathers,
can wait another day.

In Your Apple Dream

Jonathon, MacIntosh, Fuji,
and Rome don't breed true.
Baldwin, Braeburn, and Granny,
all clones, graft from the same
sweet branch of sameness,
and you begin to snore. You grunt,
partially wake, turn, and sink
to the deep pulse where the wild
gene drives this dream.

Where the brush and trees run
unruly, you kneel and paw
like a dog the living loam.
You plant each apple's
five brown seeds here and there
among the birch and alder.
Storms in your lungs blow
the rhythmic seasons along
as you weed, watch, and water.

You fence the winter animals
away. You rest, your eyes jerk,
and years pass in REM.
Like all planters, your back is sore,
and you scooch to your warm spouse
of decades. One spring, one branch
then all burst in bloom to beguile the bees,
those random pollen packers, with sap
and perfume in the mix of raw sex.

When fruiting begins, all hell
breaks loose. What you thought
were best and brightest are sour,
drought-resistant, yes, but scabby,
bug-resistant but quick to rot,
hardy but small. The remote chance
of latent sweetness may be the story
of Delicious found as a weed in a cornfield,
but mostly it's one bite, all spitters.

Mr. Appleseed's apple seeds did no better,
were grown for cider that wouldn't spoil
in winter. You toss and turn, nearly wake,
and walk the old Silk Road in Kazakhstan.
It's fall, and knobby fruit rolls beneath your feet.
The figure in robes you're following turns
as you fall in step abreast, smiles at you
and your offered apples that aren't quite right
as you stroll to the Mongol's hut in the forest.

In Your Snowflake Dream

You relax and fall with falling snow.
From dust you come, a tiny speck coated
with ice drifting fast in cirrus around a dome
of high pressure stalled over the Beaufort.

An Aleutian low with bad behavior gyres
north with enough vapor and heat
to mix things up. The H_2Os stick
and so you grow falling as snow.

It takes certain kinds of falling, cold,
and water to build on. Electricity
in your smallest parts shapes your hexagon,
and you relax, this falling into grace.

To and fro in regions of the wind
your crystal grows more ornate,
your path complex, your corners spiked,
branched, or feathered like no other.

You're falling into big country, a bench
of black spruce along the Sheenjek.
You're a smokejumper again,
and your crew is all in tuxedoes—

elegant for once. You sway down in parachutes
landing softly standing up. All OK, you sing out
your names, but from a distance they all sound
the same, wild, like geese in spring.

In My Deli Dream

You find me as you did years ago
on a bright spring day shoveling
horse manure into the pickup
for our garden of potatoes and simple salads.

I'm not a knight's squire nor peasant in rubber
boots who is quick to know I shovel paradise
for weeds, but in this dream you say again, "Stop.
The day's too nice, let's go fishing."

Still without child, we drop everything
and go, and it clouds up, and we're skunked.
We rent a cabin without fixtures or heat
and pee in the rain and mud.

In our sleeping bag rich with the history
of human sleep, we bargain and trade,
banter and barter, my little dolma,
hungry in the rich market of love.

For what your eyes do imagining us
in San Francisco, I'll be your Jamón Serrano,
your ham on *sfilatino*. For your full-bodied kiss
of house red and dip of garlic chanterelle,

accept my gorgonzola with sun-dried tomatoes
in drawn butter turmeric, salmon pâté, and prawns
in mustard Creole. So begins a little commerce
under fir rafters and drumming roof of cedar.

Too soon good dreaming dissolves on loving.
With nonsense dreams are famous for,
it turns in good taste to moose moving
on the mountain, bear swimming to our island,

the sharp and earthy odor of leaves
on the hill in the rain and even after.
It turns prodigal to the garden and child
our garden grew. Oh, let's dream it rich again,

and for your soft kiss of port, my dark-eyed partner,
and hard years as mother, I comfort you as best I can
with apples, pomegranate seeds in a blue bowl,
and something fancy, on good china this frangipani torte.

In Your Goat Dream

You are the goat leaping
through the schoolhouse window.
Hooves on tiles clickety-clack.
What heaven. Everywhere you look,
cellulose, and you, a goat.

Teacher and students gone,
the table is set with lesson plans
and open books. Math, history,
poetry, civics, and art.
What salad, what meat and potatoes.

You study the room with opalescent
eyes. Millennia in Mesopotamia
developed your stomach for this.
Bacteria in the foregut dissolving poisons,
you eat locoweed for breakfast.

Your assignment now, sane ruminant,
is happy plunder. You jump from desk
to desk, row by row, your split lip nibbling
this smorgasbord. How piquant
the aperitif of india ink spreading

its puddle on Edie's star chart.
How sweet the long division and jar
of paste. Bulletin board cork
smacks of smoky chipotle, and crayons
are red and blue and chewy.

Textbook covers are good and tough
as hill shrubs in Babylon. Homer's war,
Hundred Years' War, latest war,
the heart and brain of William Blake
make hardy fare you feed on.

Not enough, you plunge your head
in the bathroom trash for love note spitballs,
two tampons, and a roach. In the hall
you eat Teacher's silk scarf and sprinkle
little black beans on Jenny's jacket.

 When Teacher comes to chase you out,
it's your own Mrs. Peterson,
who like a goat herself makes the best
of everything. The lesson today:
Agriculture and the High Cost of Civilization.

She claps her hands. You trot back to the window,
doofus ears alert, ever the smiling Fool.
You eye her stack of Hackberry Ramblers
records and Chopin Études, still hungry.
What rutabagas, what crème brûlée!

The children turn the pages of what they're taught,
but for you it's *laissez les bon temps rouler*
with earth posters on the wall, crepe paper
turkeys, and cardboard bells, flags of desire,
all food for the great stomach of thought.

In Your Tango Dream

You're falling in love not to wake up.
Gliding to the eight count, turning
on five, guiding with a hand on her back,
nudge of a knee, thigh to thigh,
it's a difficult dance you're learning.

Head up, back straight, you embrace
the yearning heartbroken city beauty
born of the bandoneon. The wheeze and wail
of the bellows drives the push and pull
of your heart where you give and grieve.

You come from the factory with all of its pipes.
You come from the shop stopping at nothing.
Twenty years in a blink, but your hands
are clean, and your clothes explain life's bargain.
It's magic you want, and the impossible happens.

Your slight push left is central. She turns
and circles back face to face: Hello.
Step back, she follows: Don't go. Stagy
to watch, but true to the tango, you lean forward,
she back, supple as willow. Take me.

In Your Sexual Fantasy Dream

You're wide awake and doing something else.
Forty percent of the time, they say,
your mind, God help us, defaults to sex,

an endowment from a randy gene.
It is, but it's not, what you think.
You're monitoring the approach into Deadhorse.

Night, weather bad, down to a half,
gauges and needles on the mark,
your captain is flying. You call out

five hundred above minimum.
For five miles in cruise she wove lotion
in her hands, her fingers combing themselves

with lilac. One hundred above.
Her small fist walks the throttles up
increasing power just a bit.

You hear the whine; you feel the torque.

In Your Light Dream

You're always in the dark,
but the machinery of memory,
that conveyor belt working overtime,
tumbles lumens in the mind's hopper.

And here come seven musk oxen, one calf,
in the ghostly gloom of night vision
goggles as you circle overhead.
They paw the green snow of Pingok

Island, a few acres of tundra so spare
it's an ice age wonder they survive a week.
Two years on, they cross ice to the mainland,
experts at what they do, now ten.

On the cockpit infrared screen, they bunch
for protection from the bear they think you are.
Shaggy, heads out and down, only their hooves
and capes of their horns glow white hot.

In Your Prison Guard Dream

It's thumbs-up, and you are laughing
at the camera, the cute young angel
from small-town America you seem to be.

Now you're male. In dreams and war
it doesn't matter. You point to wires
clamped on a nude man's penis.

You pile the bodies high in the hall
alive and naked chained man
to man in the embrace of humiliation,

the art at which you master, this prison
your ivory tower. Though bombs may blow,
and flesh may char and hang in the street,

with your past and family far, your future dim,
you rule here in your moment of power
holding a leash tied to a madman's neck.

Revenge for revenge, there's joy in the skill
you use, this foreplay to soften him up
so he'll unhinge and tell you what you want.

Outside, what truth the papers bring
flies on pages blowing low along the street,
the only angels' wings there are.

In Your Child Soldier Dream

You belly past the goat corral
and roosting chickens. You're hungry
until the pills kick in. Now you're brave,
braver than men. Your machete
or rifle sling might catch in sorghum
leaves and rustle the spotted dog
awake, but you're a vet. You take
your time. You take care of the dog.
If you're caught and ditch the gun,
you're just a kid.

No moon, moving up wind
in dirt, you do as you're told,
do as others do. You fan out.
Two by two, hut to hut,
you sneak up and wait
on the edge of the sleepers' dreams.
Alert but quiet, nothing wild,
you know the drill.
You wait for the signal.
You're someone they count on.
You're not a difficult child.

The hands you chop
and tumble in a plastic sack
bring you food in camp,
good soldier, and praise.
Manioc is warm and comfort
on your tongue. You remember yams.
Fried plantains are sweet, and relief
rice fills. You remember meat.
Back meat, thigh meat, even arm
and heart, heat your dreams.

Sudden soccer is futbol.
You kick the round cane thing
the legless goalie throws back.
You play, you laugh, you sleep.
You scream in dreams you dream of.
If school should come, marks
on the board are beyond you.
Ball is sometimes boy, and leaf
is life. When rice is rock,
dirt is dog dead in dirt.

In Your Future Dream

You're probably dead
but going on much like yourself,
sans body hair, well thought of,

a smooth sort of ghost. Just being around
was once a kind of love.
Pawing and pestering were another.

Nothing hurts you now. Signs of age
may show but inside never.
Yet machinery there,

bad bushing, worn sprocket,
slipped a chain,
and the chain broke.

You live, if you live,
as thought or soul or sigh
or window fog on someone's drive

to work. You haunt the hills
and valleys of ballads,
each chord change at the bridge,

and the high note redemptions in opera:
Miss Butterfly in heartbreak,
Samson bringing down the house.

You might ride a movie score under fire.
The fall of Somoza, let's say, cycle of fear,
sad love, marimbas, and the pan flute's

breathy ascension take you
to the Managua you recall and cities
of the world the world becomes.

So little soul to go around, you recycle
as the kid stuck in traffic everywhere,
and traffic always takes you in.

You push the looted swivel chair
on caster wheels
loaded with bags of rice,

or you're rich and push the bike
or motorbike that won't run stacked
six feet high in back with laundry.

Clouds might rain the smog away.
It might rain a month or more.
Your hair grows back.

You're stuck in traffic,
traffic loves you,
and you'd like to fix that chain.

In Your Tie Dream

Your son grows taller in your arms
as you stand behind reaching around
looking over his shoulder at your faces
in the mirror. The image, a before
and after, is far too clear.

Sound asleep, you and the world
know that tying a tie, like the left turn
in traffic, is one of the more difficult things
you do in life. Asleep, awake, the ways
of the world we drill in dreams.

Your son in your arms, you begin
the procedure. Here is the short
narrow end, and here is the long
wider end with diagonal stripes.
Now comes crossing over, curling under,

coming up to your chin over your fingers
holding the beginning knot, now down
your Adam's apple, curving right,
crossing over, switching hands,
curling under, up, then down inside the bight.

Now snug it up. All that fuss and only
a slipknot to make a gentleman. As a kid
with a leather tie, you cinched a saddle
to a young bull and rode with enough imagination
to make him a proper horse.

There are many ties. Some are rep,
Foulard, paisley, and the tie that's a fish.
Last summer paddling the canoe, your son
tied a half hitch in the water with each
strong stroke. You lower your arms.

Tall, sixteen, well-knotted, yourself before,
the stranger you raised glides away.

In Your Retirement Dream

for Ted Pope

You're making a living in Mexico
or in the mountains or on a sailboat
running downwind wing on wing.

At last, every idea is personal.
All meetings are adjourned, no publish
or perish, at least not yet, bullshit.

If you flew the CEO from airport to airport
in the corporate jet, now you putt-putt
lake to lake with da Vinci in your head.

If you painted color-compression abstracts,
critics reviewed your shows in Cuba,
New York, and Taiwan but never bought.

Now they queue with cash for figured scenes
of where you live: a woman, your wife,
playing cards at a yellow tilted table. It's a cage

you open, and you let this cheetah run.

I Got a Sawzall

Melting Pot

It's gusting fifty when I taxi the Goose off the beach.
She waddles over stones in the shallows then settles
into the swell taking on the full load of her belly. This time
it's nine Samoans, each wide as a hatch cover on a freighter.
Somehow all the monkey motion of pistons in concert barking
Baroque plows us through spray, up on the step, and then into air.
The great wheel of a low driving up from the gulf carries
and clobbers us over a ridge along with blasts from speakers
on a processor in the bay. "Take another piece of my heart out,
baby," Lady Joplin squalls. Injured love, sleet, pollen from Japan,
and iffy transport over the islands conflate. That night Icelanders
off a crabber and my crew mix it up at the hotel. Upstairs next door
I hear moaning, a child with an earache? It's her mother, the barmaid,
our leggy darling, whimpering at the height of her powers.

Ice Road Trucker

"The more I do other stuff, the more I like trucking."
Because she's pretty it works, and they put her on TV.
Reality looking good entertains you, me, and the dummy
next door. Producers riding along, aware of tracking
polls, ask dumb questions. What's this thing
for? She's not so pretty some say. Look, crooked teeth,
bunny boots, work gloves, sweatshirt, and fleece
jacket. We're not fooled. The beauty's in the machine.
There's the clutch and here's the stick. She will belch
her diesel and crank those double-axel drivers
high and low, hooking tons of manifest past switch
backs, no guardrails, gear by gear. When stuck we love her
chaining up down on her knees. "I also like painting my nails,"
she says, and we love her, the snowy hills, the miles and miles.

Paul Austin: Oilfield Pianist

Brilliant with clinkers, your Bach scrambles through camp,
romping through security, spark room, and mess hall,
tinkling through incident command. For three hours, five
if you're lucky, you practice your passion nightly in the hallway,
keeping elbows loose, in coveralls and cap. No one knows
quite what you do on shift with computers down in materials.
Your fingers play there, too, dispensing pallets of valves fortissimo,
lowboys of ninety-foot stem, jet fuel, and gross lots of gloves adagio,
those Green Apes and Happy Harry's we're happy to wear.
We need protection from our own mistakes with subs and pipes
that bite, big boxes, steel banding, and the flange that bites.
We are the brutes of heave, shove, and slam,
but you play, and we hear you late in our little rooms.
We hear you in central files and on the shuttle home.

Videographer

"So this is what I do when I'm not around,"
and he sends a couple pictures of himself
surrounded by computers and a mixing board.
We look over one shoulder and then the other
seeing only the merest angle of his brow, cheek,
and jaw lit by the screens, knowing him mostly by blood,
memory working out our full-frontal son.

The wonders of wide angle dimly reveal balcony
seats to each side and the glow of a woman
in a bare back gown checking her smartphone,
itself a lesser source of light. The stage below repeats
and repeats one bright beauty after another on the screens.
Like a NASA shuttle launch, the mystery moves
for man at the controls, man in the dark.

Why these pictures validate his life, or kind of do,
he doesn't know, but we remember him playing in boxes,
making shadows, shining a light. Scene dissolving
into scene, light line along hip line, the gold
glow of a rolling shoulder, sheath spangle
and flash, the arms reaching into focus,
he loves being the guy in control, guy in the dark.

Intermission

About my Hamlet the less said, the better.
In the Scottish play I overplayed my promotion,
but classmates okayed my hour as strutter and fretter.
My costar washed her hands and bloodied the ocean,
or so we imagined, the words big and small
convincing our minds of murder. None doubted
the guilt, fog, or geography while I waited for my call
backstage sweating and itchy in my doublet.
We made our bows to faint applause then plunged
into our daily work, swimming in media, the flood
of war, floods, rape, and trade. Mortality hung
on our lumps. We prick our fingers for a blink of blood.
We go to the bathroom, we marry now and then,
and ghosts we see neither speak nor beckon.

Weatherman Healing

for Bob Scarbrough

"Left turn birds," he calls them,
the phalaropes spinning for bugs
on the tundra pond by the hangar.
Adults long gone to probably Mexico,
the young are left working plankton
up in a whorl from the shallows.

Step outside and it smells like fall.
Ice any day. How do they find their way?
It doesn't follow they wouldn't follow.
Is survival non-sequitur? But all
he says is, "Here on the water,
some turn right, more so in Chile."

Late at night when little that's good begins,
he drives again and again from coast to coast,
his war bride of thirty years beside him
shooting rolls of film: window glare, cactus,
cowboys, her foot, each motel. For modesty's
sake she eats her kimchi in the street.

This year when spring flew north
with all its geese and leaves, she died.
Now he works overtime not to go home,
his house a house of houseplants limp and leggy,
schefflera needing water, dipnets in the shed,
boat outside on its trailer all tarped over.

Some mornings promise busy work,
dry runs for the day to day, some day
the real thing. "Look here, Mr. Mirror,"
he says, shaving by instinct right jaw first.
"The herb for winter is oatmeal
in your shoes, good for the skin."

Back to work, he takes flight plans
for local flights. What joke, what cure
there is in weather he takes hourly:
wind something, pressure and sky something,
and temps he feels squinting west
into the face of Asia naming cold

as best he can with smaller
and smaller then negative numbers.

Take an Orange in Case You Get Lost

Half throttle for breakaway power gets you rolling.
Tires stiff and flat on the bottom thump
for a hundred feet until they round out
by the runway for the machines we use
to move us along into our dark day's work.

Seat cushions get hard, snow squeaks
under feet and wheels. High-tech parkas
crackle like shopping bags. Noon twilight,
heavy on the blues, pretty much says it all.
It pays to have a past you can use.

The ball of the world, for example, rolling under
the sun, and the furniture of wind
pushed into the corners, rivers running,
and all the flyers plus swans coming in
with the grace of snow to mate, nest, and feed.

Your good money bringing the menu and a tanker
out back with a three-inch hose pumping a liter
of house red. Art, language, agriculture.
O the pizza, the pasta, the whole grilled fish,
and your one and only strolling in with the gift of fire.

Siping

"Designing snow tires is a black art,
and the goddamn Finns do it best,"
my sort-of-friend from work, the kind
we all have, says. At every chance
he talks rally racing or hating Arabs,
but this one time his wisdom
on tread siping is bias I can use.

I mount my winter rims with Hakkapeliittas,
and I'm pleased with the generous spelling
of their name, the rich rubber smell
of Africa, the thought of the high-tech,
frozen-lake test track. I jack the car one wheel
at a time, putting her new shoes on.
I snug up the lugs, tight but not too tight.

What ornate tracks we'll make of inscrutable
medieval Latin in the snow of our going
around corners. No smudging offline for us,
we hope, on Deadman's Curve going downhill,
no blurring to a stop on winter's white pages,
backing out of garages or parking spaces,
slowing for the walker, true believer, or infidel.

The tires will crunch their skinny letters,
printing double columns on the snowy roads,
gripping what they can to move us
in our common round from home to the work
we work so hard at and back. It's code
we hope the troopers won't ever have to read,
skid and swerve to broken bones in bags of blood.

I torque the last lugs. This little job reminds me
of the Gutenberg Museum guide pointing
to her name tag's double letters. "I'm Riitta,
the Finn. We believe in something extra."
She calls on me to pull the lever of the great man's
machine. "Hard, harder," and off comes
a page of Isaiah, some of my best work.

Distaff

Excavation for the new hangar begins.
A scratcher machine loosens
frozen gravel; and two loaders scoop,
back up, pivot, climb out of the hole
where the slab will go, go to a pile,
dump, and return. The drivers' orange-
and-yellow safety vests sparkle
in the work lights and dark.

It's that old industrial rumba they do,
and you can almost hear Bebo Valdes
in his nineties at the piano, his syncopated
"El Manicero" dancing down the wind.
Standing there in our parkas with Bebo,
we see one driver has pigtails,
and we like the way she dumps her bucket.

Truth and beauty come around
and around taking care of things.
My home systems manager
prepares our taxes and cleans
the Augean stables of my mind.
Other women belly along on rafters,
checking insulation in our attic.
They smile and drill my root canals.

And this morning doing her preflight,
Abie in coveralls climbs the rotor mast
of the helicopter checking for oil leaks
while two surveyors strap in
before setting off like Lewis and Clark
to measure things all for the taking.

All we know, all we need to know
for now, is that she reaches up
like Miss Liberty lighting the world
for some, Sacajawea with a broken heart
pointing to the great mountains,
checking safety wire and cotter pin
in the Jesus nut that holds it all together.

Encephalogram

The hunter waits at the breathing hole,
ice underfoot, wind in his fur,
his mind, the mind of an auditor.

The dim glow inside the back of his head
is mostly one thought: Water welling up.
Frontal, temporal, cubical after cubical,

you'd swear there's not a light on
in the whole place. Above winter's
spreadsheet, mind flickers in the wind

with hunger and the usual worries:
money for fuel, strontium in the lichen,
boys at war, babies on Coke.

Mere thought idling cold in boredom
monitors the sun minting
his gold and the moon her silver.

Eventually lightning resting in readiness
will fire the brain to strike, harpoon,
he hopes, a hundred pounds of meat.

Eventually idea freighted with heavy
metal is seal coming up for air
making one of the mistakes it takes to live.

And always the sun and the moon
in the skull of heaven spending
their millions one coin at a time.

Florina Sings *Die Loreley*

Ich weiss nicht, was soll es bedeuten,
Das ich so traurig bin
—HEINE

I do not know what my sadness means
nor why halfway down this Franconian wine
bottle my heart breaks, only that Florina
in a red dress sings an old story in Rüdesheim.

In firm German, a sharp bend above Koblenz
churns the current and makes a standing wave
with hydraulics. An alluring blonde on a cliff sings,
and boatmen distracted with what they can't have

smack rocks and die. I have fallen in fast water
myself where singing nearly pulled me down.
What little boats I steered rolled awash in the rip.
Ripe roundness in the turn of the bilge and tumble home

stem--so sleek to swim, so full to haul
on shore. If lucky enough to hear steep scenery
comb shadows in a mermaid's hair, you don't want
the boat you ride to look like machinery.

Night after night Florina sweetly plows
her lines along, working desire into the verses,
making the world worth mourning when we fall,
worth praising when we float with forces

of nature, love, or just rivers. Wild salmon gone,
the Rhine is tame now with locks and bow-thruster
boats, but under a roof so lit by Christmas lights it's seen
from space the singing work goes on at Winzerkeller.

Three Weeks Rain

Broccoli bolts, and the cabbage split their heads.
Slugs steering along on trails of snot
eat buckshot holes in their food and ours

feeding themselves and soon those little lives
in the soil. Surely we're standing upon
a symbiotic frenzy of microbial Calcuttas.

Surely we're more than gardeners visiting
in the rain, dripping from nose and chin,
oohing and aahing over stalks and blooms

with Charlene. Retired, thirty-three years
clerical with the Anchorage Police Department
typing reports, tabulating mayhem—

all those women discarded in the brush
beside the roads, busted wives on the phone,
cabbies slumped behind the wheel,

and alienated kids drifting the migrant malls
bulldozed in twenty years for box stores
bulldozed in ten, rubble on rubble.

Time now to stake and baby her flowers.
"The seed catalogs all know me," she says,
and she orders her tubers with a warning:

"Visible eyes, or I send them back."
Servant of the seasons, she pots her starts,
transplants, and if they don't bloom she winters

them over. "I never give up on a dahlia."
And into the mulch of the great world's litter
they go again where from time to time we all stir.

I Got a Sawzall

because a man ran around on his wife,
and she, now his ex, sold me a marriage-full
of the good stuff junked in the garage
pennies on the dollar. Table saw, chop saw,
drills galore, nifty kit of wrenches clipped
in descending order of size, so shiny so bright,
an airless paint sprayer with pistol grip,
battery-operated caulking gun (who knew?),
and pistol grip of course, ladder, kneepads
and, sweet mother of Jesus, the Sawzall.

Christmas in July, the wreckage of marriage
home improvement tools with attachments
for your every desire. Our old microwave died,
and my wife bought a new one (has a button
just for popcorn), but the old backing plate
was a bitch and wouldn't come off the wall.
Big molly bolts in tight quarters wouldn't budge.
Well, you hoist up that big baby, bend the blade
at a 45 angle, squeeze the trigger
like a .50 cal, and cut them off at the knees.

Dust, noise, vibration, Sturm and Drang,
cursing, problem-solving the American way.
Men call it man's work. Thus, we imagine
ourselves domestic heroes. You see us around,
a Solomon or two in T-shirt and jeans.
Your horned herds, your gamboling lambs,
bubbling fountains, your lilies of the field—
they do not toil, neither do they spin.
And with only hair for raiment, my love smiles
into bed with all she needs for fixing heaven.

Against Indifference

Just Between Us

I have the perfect face for melting
into a crowd. Muddy green eyes,
potato nose, some foggy hair
clouding my El Capitan half dome.

I could be a spy, a mole, that quiet drinker
at the bar. I give the effect of tan wallpaper
in a dental office, empty African savannah,
possible but unlikely lions in grass behind the chair.

North Slope oil workers mistake me for air,
cold wind on the face, just outside of where
the mind wanders: fishing the Kenai, mother humming
a little something, rubbing clove on a toothache.

Women let me stare at beauty they hardly know
they own, fingernails clicking meaning into keyboards,
or shucking hillside corn, baby in a sling,
sun scorching caramel on their arms.

There I am dozing on the chicken bus
or commuter train, my face in dappled
shadow, our dusty fraternity nodding off
dreaming against indifference.

In the lobby on a cell phone, that's me turning
away for a fraction to whisper of love or work.
Sometimes for me you hold the elevator,
sometimes I lift your bucket full from the well.

Some Fogs

I ask around and most agree the Lady
of the Lake rises like radiation fog
from cold water chilling and condensing
overnight the air above. When temperature
and dew point meet, she wears a diaphanous
gown and moves like furniture on rollers, Anglo,
voluptuous and cruel, beguiling boaters,
pilots, and wandering knights in love.

Advection fog comes from elsewhere.
It's the northeast wind, Inuit sea smoke
off pack ice in a rush of mukluks onshore,
that drops temps thirty degrees and drives
back North Slope mosquitoes
giving caribou some relief.
It's the moist gray fur pushing upslope
into the Rockies, good hiding
for history-hidden women
picking berries in fall.
It's the cool flow
off Michigan invading the Loop.
This is the one with cat's feet.

The international protocol
for aviation weather reporting
lumps freezing fog with ice fog.
They're not the same,
as we in the Arctic know,
and we blame the French
who, like officious difficult friends,
won't see in fog what is
when you tell it like it is.

For reasons of trade,
those great Bordeaux
and cloudy tons of lingerie
the world thinks we live for,
and for another grand alliance
in a new crusade we die for,
we allow reports with BR
(short for *brouillard*) meaning mist
(falling droplets, visibility $5/8$ mile plus)
and FU (*fumeé*) meaning smoke,
meaning the usual war somewhere,
forests burning, oranging the sun
for over-the-pole cargo planes.

No, freezing fog is just frozen fog,
official, Gaullist and gloomy, no exit,
up and down and all around.
I think instead of old Matisse shaking
with palsy, dropping the brush, picking up
the scissors to make with civilizing cuts
the nudes and leaves we love.
Only by contrivance with artifice
do the delicate instruments of homing
lead us out always a little lost enough
for discovery, as walking is controlled falling,
a kind of failing forward into the clear.

Ice fog, I mean to say, is ice crystals
needle-shaped and suspended vertically.
Your steps crunch in the pale pall
of minus twenty. You look up
in daylight and see the low lemon sun,
fuzzy and flanked by sun dogs.

In the dark, straight up, stars stare,
northern lights waver,
and plane lights pulse.

Those galleons bear our bullets and beans
and recordings by the stack of Django Reinhardt,
who lost the use of two fingers in a fire
and found a new way to fret and run the guitar.
Some nights he plays forever his Gypsy jazz
with lambent licks fast and sure on "Lady Be Good."
He swings with the wounded hand of man.

If you're flying in ice fog on approach,
weary traveler, merchantman, knight errant,
the crude hand on the yoke always correcting is yours.
On the gauges, you scan with a subtle eye.
Perhaps you'll glance below and see the small circle
of tundra following you all the way in.
At the last second the runway's lights
will open her sparkling arms and see you home.
Trust me. I know my fogs.

Some Gossip

She slipped in a gas station and tore
her face open on a lube rack.
Poor thing, what was she thinking?

The neighbor found him delirious in bed.
He'd soiled himself. Too weak to reach
the phone, dog barking, now he's dead.

She got this thing for the kids' ski coach
and moved out while her husband was sick.
And the kids? The kids act oblivious.

Ever alert to the human condition,
our own Greek chorus, we stand aside
and comment and somehow bind the tribe

with know-it-all judgments, scandal, or shock.
What smidgen of empathy we have we trot
along with irony and love on our best little zingers.

This airport security guard found a vibrator
in her bag. He took it out, held it up (passion's,
not terror's, reasonable facsimile), and turned it on.

Boys with machine guns were hosing down
the crowd. In the ditch he hid in, three baby ducks
were pecking rot from a dead man's leg. Baby ducks.

Some Colors

This idea we have of yellow—ripe
banana in a basket, soft-boiled egg yolk
cooling in a bowl, the sunrise blowing
its long trombone across the bay—
is all about blue, which is missing.

It's light alone, all colors, high noon,
altogether colorless, makes white blank.
Lose the blue, no matter that unstable
tan or khaki muddies the mind's eye,
and the light that's left is yellow-yellow.

No ideas but in the colors of things.
See how black-eyed Susans, buttercups,
and tansies play along the porch? Better yet,
here phlegm coughed chartreuse, and pale
green splotched on floral sheets looks bilious.

For the general ache of existence at midnight
Monk gave us blues wandering around in G.
Some sung sorrows are blue, filtered funky, funny,
or plaintive as "Corina" with love's hard times. Hurt
pride just cries in the line "I got a bird that whistles."

But here, it's my guess, blood washed clean
from terra cotta tiles misted with Luminall
will luminesce a splatter cringing in the dark.
Out in the garden that oxeye daisy, reluctant
witness, Kabuki face bowing in the breeze,

must have seen it all, masking all
white in thought: the crushing of the grass,
the tan boot skidding on the ochre earth,
and the soft falling of the yellow scarf
that brings the telltale semen to the scene.

Some String

At some point you'll ask how much string
in life do I need? Will the disheveled
wad in a junk drawer and some wraps
I wound on a popsicle stick in the garage

somewhere pay out too soon?
When I was a boy and we were farmers
bailing wire was such a resource
and binder twine was everywhere.

Balls of it, rolls of it, hanks hung on nails—
feed sacks snugged up in miller's knots,
homemade calf halters, nosering reins
for the bull I used to ride until he was two.

In schoolbooks then a half-bull ate folks
in a labyrinth, and a bright fellow trailing
string stalked and safely killed him. Bright
because a woman gave him a clew.

Only a gardener now, what string I need
ties dahlias to their stakes or cinches
plywood to the cartop roof rack.
On walks I walk the dog without a leash

and she comes at a gallop when I call,
and every day a bright woman hands me a line
I trail back home in the forest tree by tree
looped in love one bowline after another.

Some Women's Hair

Where I look, I see a woman's head.
Or more exactly, I see her brown hair
and part of her neck because she is looking
down at something she is writing,
a letter about kayaking with sea otters
swimming on their backs holding their babies.
A silver earring with a tiny bear paw,
only four toes though bears have five,
of inlaid turquoise sways along the subtle
muscles of her neck. She writes now about small
waves of plankton soup slapping the hull.

Women in other rooms of other years
wore their hair differently. It hung
long and lank from blondes, brunettes,
and the ones' whose hair was black
but have no special name here.
Some hair was always covered
in public with scarves of many names.
Some hair was short or corn-rowed
or braided or even buzz cut
or was gray, usually short,
or white tinted blue, or any color
and stiff with stuff they sprayed it with.

Sombok used to cut my hair.
She would lean me back first
on the sink to shampoo. I remember
so well how she bent to her work
and was so beautiful and near
with her glossy black hair. I asked her
how to count to ten in Korean,
which she taught, but I forgot.

Lush afros you don't see anymore.
I remember Barbara scratching her head
with her slender middle finger.
Her hand would cock back like a cobra
above her black halo then strike precisely
with her unpainted fingernail
making only a slight disturbance
to the ringlet jungle going in all the way
to the scalp. Her earrings, big brass hoops,
caught light and jangled against the collar
of her red blouse when she argued about boys,
practically babies, fighting war after war.

I remember the pick combs of red
and green you used to see in hip pockets
going down the street and the regular combs
spilling out from messy purses at school.
A teacher, once, gave us all fine-toothed combs
to clean out the nits and lice,
arthropods common to the poor.

Grandmother Olga in the fifties wore
a bun stuck with combs of tortoise shell,
but mornings when she rose from sleep
her hair hung loose and long.
She combed and combed the electricity there,
and if it were winter and still dark,
I couldn't help but watch
to see the sparks of fire that crackled
like thought from women everywhere
right there in her hands.

Eclipse

In memory of Ray Charles

An ex-president falls,
and the news burns sunny
with a week of words
pictures and print
blinding and confining
as a child's capture in a closet.

A crack of light
boxes the dead door
blocking the sun
and song
of Ray's "Georgia"
rising on my mind
out there.

Dog Dancing

The collie up on two hind legs barking,
the farm woman laughing and holding
his paws turning one two-two one two-two
around and around the yard on last year's
grass in the sharp March sun with the wind
blowing her white apron and red print skirt
in a twirl, his rough blond coat rippling,
tail cranking. How they whirled themselves dizzy
past garden beds and mats of blue crocus
in their fuzzy cups of silver and the tulips
poking purple-green tongues through dirt
and mulch sixty years ago, Mother and Laddy
dancing the Dog Dance Polka, with me galloping
along in the wind and sun demanding my turn.

Coccyx

Rear leg bones in whales, front legs in snakes—
hidden, here comes the past along for the ride.
Mother brushed burrs from my pants and wiped
dirt from my cherry cheeks so elders would take
no notice. We sidestepped to our seats in the pew,
not a sign of the fight-or-flight fit I threw before church.
The burning towers fell, now travelers slouch
through worthless screening trading shame as proof
we're safe. ID'd, scanned, or groped for bombs
tweezers, or lotion, we swim more or less smoothly
through theaters of fear. Low among the leaves,
we breed and self-select to slither who used to run.
Anthologies of bones we sit on, appendices of useless guts,
to climb and swing for man we hiss and scribble sonnets.

Pall Bearers

Shadows in the foyer condense to a woman who knows just
what to do. She's small, wears black of course, and one hand
cups the other in the professional pose of not standing out.

She sorts us by size: big, medium big, bigger. We follow
her out to the hearse down chapel steps like obedient
retrievers tracking the beautiful balls of her heels.

She rolls the casket halfway out, and we clump around.
One with a torn rotator cuff switches sides, but she keeps
us moving and smiles us into position for the lift

which must be level up stairs, around doors, and in.
There's no ignoring the weight. The shrunken woman
we imagine inside also smiling has this little job in mind,

and we bend to this work and honor, clumsy but careful.
Her face, the priest says composing his, was the map
of Ireland. We wipe our eyes and sniff or laugh

as stories from son and sister lead along her life
from birth, family, something about work, and now this.
Soon the professionals and organ lead us with this load

of transfiguration, but it's slow going for us, out
and down the steps. Death may be light, but not
the box it goes in, and we are such beginners.

So One Day

you're cleaning a drawer, and there you are:
old address books, love letters, letters of loss.
Our son's drawings unfold on a beach of sleeping
elephant seals on a good day he captured well.
Birthday cards celebrate what I've become,
venerable Neanderthal, skeptical Visigoth.

Business cards composting from years of work
address the little their owners stood for.
Yin and yang of rejection, acceptance slips.
Buzz words buzz in and out, off the rim.
The future pivots, and the past attempts a rebound.
Rubber bands, sticky notes, so much mulch.

Our stories and the world's are used again
and again like a preowned car. The little man
in a plaid jacket skating backward on the river
in our heads cuts and curves each bend
of recycled versions we bit and bought.
Life is hard but good and getting better.

Time goes about its business making slots
for things to happen. Leaders we choose
speak poorly or well driving us to economies
and wars that cost a fortune. People die.
Dumb luck and ok genes charm the lucky
to fall in love and lie in love's long limbs.

Slow learners some, a starter marriage
or two, mistakes parenting seems to require—
it takes a while to learn the workaday
maintenance of that love. Blessed relief,
we dig now into something that works and puts
energy into everything much like the sun.

Outside, swallows sweep in June's long light
and tulips open by six or close softly
if clouds convene. Worms and fungi feed
in principalities of bloom and demolition, grist
for generation celebrated in garden columns
and here, perhaps, in summer's song.

I throw half the mess out and close the drawer.
Failure to complete is at least a start. Philosophers
at heart, we learn to walk by falling down,
and the future sprouts in the past tangling up
like peas and chickweed. I go to the garden
to find what's growing there and growing in me.

Ugly Lovers

making whoopee in the dark contend
with latent beauty, grunt by grunt, groan
by groan, on a level playing field equally blind,
each a black blank. Hips and hills, blankets
bunched in glory, legs and arms, fractals
that branch and branch, the slow work of birth
begins with a shiver in the sensate nerve.

Let us praise now the misshapen,
the roly poly, the puffy, the boney,
snaggled, pocked, hairy-backed,
flat-chested, beer-bellied, bald, knock-
kneed, weak-chinned, wall-eyed wonder
of us. Praise now the gutsy art of desire
in the bowlegged bull and cow of us.

Wheelbarrow me to the dance under the tree
by the tavern. Turn around, turn around,
bark shins, stub toes, eat chicken, and steal
my watch. Barf in a barrel and call me honey.
If painters paint us show the brushstrokes, bristle
tracks, and thumb smudge, our nicks and knocks.
Let mudslide oils beget our boys and girls.

Winter Garden

We wake and raise the shades to this news just in:
Area Gardens Grow Deep and White. Leavening
windrows bulge like dough. We start coffee and TV.
Next up, video of someone's dead in roadside rows.

Our gardens grow very well this year.
The plump beds, parallel and clinical white,
swell and nearly fill our vegetable ward
with the advance of the season.

Straight from space, cold snaps set us back as usual.
These we accept, shrugged off like lies in high places.
Thaws in April we thought normal as taxes
soon hardened hanging from eaves and fences.

We know that little things work overtime
to make a living. Even now under clotted leaves,
herding bacteria into a digestive embrace,
slime mold yellow as dog vomit creeps along.

Gestating bulbs of tulips and daffodils swell.
Rhubarb, ruby red and vaguely penile,
nudges upward like thought in the loam,
the usual brilliant idea coming slowly to mind.

Nearly May, the bird feeder heaped with conehead
snow surveils the buried rows of calm and this airy
mulch. On each fence post a space shuttle stands tall
ready to launch, melt, or, like peace, postpone.

Morning Paper

Seven women walk the world's edge
in the long shot on the back page.
It says they're hunting wood and water.
Sure enough, dust and wind water
the eye if you look too close. Buckets
and bundles on their heads make them tall.
Shawls flapping yellow, they look like flowers
you finger paint sloppy in first grade.

Perhaps that seven is six or nine—
and Betty West, too young and pretty
for a critic, never liked your art, the work
and play it is, its dribble dribble.
Dogs loved as blobs chasing crows
scribbled in turbulent flight smudged
a messy meaning none too clear—
nothing like Ida Olson's kittens.

Now snow squalls water the eye
as blurry women shimmer to wood
and water. Nothing like rime and grit
to bring the banter of Sudan. The chinook
gusting, our roof vents rattle with laughter.
That chatter goads the footsore to fix
meals for their kids and deal, what now,
with what on earth they must be thinking.

Somewhere laser drones sparkle a target,
but it's the lifting of buckets and bundles,
the rain that never comes or comes too hard
that cools the coffee while women are shot
walking into news. Ambushed in a line
or two, it takes the work of words to keep
them moving to wood and water. It takes
the wind and fabric slapping their limbs.

DAVID MCELROY lives in Anchorage, Alaska and recently retired as a commercial pilot of small planes in the Arctic in support of wildlife research, industry, and wild fire control. He has two previous books of poems, *Making it Simple* and *Mark Making*.